PREPARING PARENTING MINDSET FOR FUTURISTIC LEARNING

DR DHEERAJ MEHROTRA

Contents

Preface

Preparing Parenting Mindset For Futuristic Learning is a step toward making parents aware of their qualities to harness the skills of their wards in the best possible manner. It enhances motivational skills and re-visits the way parenting should happen.

Post CORONA, we all have seen the change in the mindset of the children, and hence this type of re-visit on parenting is essential.

Happy Reading.

Cheers!

www.authordheerajmehrotra.com

ONE

Preparing the Parents Pefectly

Parents used common strategies to manage parenting difficulties, including doing family activities together and keeping in touch with family/friends. The new-age parenting targets an approach toward treating them as young adults.

Quality Parenting is the need of the hour. As a result, at the same time, the boards of education and learning must develop a plan to help schools, teachers, and parents educate children about safe, responsible use of the Internet. For example, encourage schools and families to place computers in shared rooms (such as family rooms, dining rooms, offices or libraries), where children can use the Internet with others around them. And teach children never to share personal information (name, address, telephone, or credit card number) online. This may go a long way in making this a success. The day-to-day activities at the school and the home education will provide a healthy liking for the computer. This is required to foster appropriate Internet use-schoolers and other young children.

It is also a debating fact that despite the increasing use of computers in elementary schools, there hasn't been a decrease in the formal teaching of penmanship. The children use just as much paper as before computers became a classroom standard. Hence, one must keep in mind that writing with a pencil involves an equally important set of skills like typing on a keyboard.

Exposure to the Internet can help preschoolers and children in the early elementary grades master literacy and other cognitive skills and spur the integration of these skills early in their development. Parents and school leaders who look for online opportunities for younger children can be guides to engaging, age-appropriate content. The Internet can reinforce everyday learning opportunities and be a powerful tool for fostering interaction among adults and young children. It takes much to conduct a new means of knowledge in this regard. The task of the teaching gentry must ponder regarding computing of this sort; they must help teachers, parents, and children use the Internet more effectively for learning. For example, they ought to suggest education-related websites for parents and children to visit together - and give them learning activities to do once they get there. Offer education-related help for students online, like after-school tutoring.

Provide teachers with professional development opportunities to help them model effective use of the Internet as a tool for students' learning, including integrating Internet learning with traditional classroom learning. If teacher training takes place outside of regular school hours, offer teachers incentives to participate. If teacher training pulls teachers out of the classroom, parents should be made to know why it is essential to support this professional development. The Internet users to communicate more effectively with parents and students goes a long way toward generating interest for all. For instance, launch school district or school websites or publicise websites in newsletters and places where parents are likely to be. Update websites frequently with relevant, timely information. Post exemplary student work online, with teacher commentary explaining why this work meets academic standards. Make websites interactive by soliciting comments or holding public forums about education issues online. Encourage teachers, parents, and students to communicate through email, make their email IDs and even share off-line with that reference to generate pulses of craze and interest in being a netizen. And finally, engage the community. This can be quickly done by buying computer and Internet training classes for parents or hosting convenient opportunities for parents, community leaders, librarians, teachers, and others to talk together about children's use of the Internet. Schools may want to collaborate with libraries, community computing centres, local colleges and universities, and other places offering alternative computers.

It is high time to dwell more and become DIGITALLY sound to understand the new generation. Remind yourself that you're a good parent doing your best in a challenging situation by celebrating the small victories each day.

Happy Parenting!

The following are ways we can help parent them with delight!

Secret # 1
Believe in PARENTING Power! Enjoy the blessing you have received as a PARENT.
Be proud and stay Fit! A GOOD PARENTING CAUSES HEADACHES, BUT BAD PARENTING CAUSES HEARTACHES

Secret # 2
Get ready for the most challenging job: Parenting is the most demanding job that you have ever done or will be doing. Get ready to learn the tricks of the trade. Be prepared for different situations.

Secret # 3
Lean "how to do caring for the baby" Parenting begins from pregnancy. Once you are pregnant, you will have to stop smoking and drinking. You have to avoid tea and coffee. You need to eat healthy food, get enough rest and so on.

Secret # 4

Learn from experienced parents: If you are a first-time parent, there is so much to learn from people who have already raised kids. Your parents can teach you so many things.

Secret # 5
Learn to Stop complaining: Your child may not follow you, but this does not mean you should start complaining. When you make complaints, your child's ego will be hurt.
A good parent loves their child for who they are, not who they will be.

Secret # 6
Keep your expectations high: You should always have high expectations about your child; this will boost confidence in your child. Good parent allows their children to be responsible for their behaviour.

Secret # 7
Encourage your child to take reasonable risks: Risk-taking is suitable for personal development; you should encourage your child to take appropriate risks. We must treat our kids as our equals and not as subordinates.

Secret # 8
Don't react immediately: When your child makes mistakes, don't react immediately. AnalyzeAnalyse the situations thoroughly before you respond. Love your child no matter what. No one is perfect; we have all made mistakes and will continue to.

Secret # 9
Give your children appropriate ways to feel powerful. Let your kid do his struggle: Struggle is a vital mantra to succeed in life, don't make things easier for the child.

Secret # 10
Keep everything real: Don't lie to your child; let him understand how things are in the real world. If your child is testing you through.... A temper tantrum, anger, crying, disrespect.... It is best to leave the room and tell him to talk to him later.

Secret # 11
Listen to your kids: When your kid wants to say something, don't ignore him. Stop what you are doing and actively listen to him. Don't interrupt; express your opinion only after he

stops. Be firm YET kind!

Secret # 12
Talk to your child: Don't wait for your child to strike the communication. Ask him questions, and encourage him to ask a question.
MOM & DAD: "Do not compare me to other children consistently; it makes me jealous."

Secret # 13
Be communicative: Always find time for communication, and never disconnect your kid's call. Communication helps you understand your child and helps him understand his parent.

Secret # 14
Show Good Judgment: Teach what is right and what is wrong. Make them follow the right things and avoid doing wrongs. Never try to motivate your child by withdrawing your love.

Secret # 15
Stick to Your Rules: You should stick to these rules when you make a rule. If you don't follow the rules, how can you expect your child to

follow the rules? Never give in to pleas, tears, demands or pouting.

Secret # 16
Become a role model: If you want your kid to be good, you should be a good person yourself. The kids are always watching you, never doing anything wrong in front of them.

Secret # 17
Control your emotions: If you express extreme emotions (anger, frustrations etc.) in front of your child, your child is likely to copy that (believe me, children are good at imitating).

Secret # 18
Let them imitate: Human beings learn by imitation; imitation is the first learning method. Encourage skill development through imitation.

Secret # 19
Show Love: Children are not very good at deciphering the meaning behind words. Therefore, a simple "I love you" does not mean

anything to them. Show them your love through hugs, kisses, and even gifts.

Secret # 20
Be positive: If you are positive, your child will grow into an optimist individual. You might fail at something; however, don't should your failures.
Mom & Dad: " Simply correct my mistakes instead of yelling at me."

Secret # 21
Avoid negativity: If you are a negative person, your child might grow into a pessimistic individual. If you show your positive side, your child will not incorporate negativity.

Secret # 22
Make them feel secure: Your child should understand you as a haven. They need to feel confident around you. Let your child feel that he is safe with you.

Secret # 23
Build trust: If you want your child to rely on you, you should build trust. If he shares his secret, don't reveal it to anyone, not even your partner.

Secret # 24
Reflect on your experience: Your childhood experience can help you in your parenting journey. If there were things that you liked, implement those things. If you had a bad experience, avoid those things.

Secret # 25
Share your life experience: The child can learn so many things from you as parents. Tell your kids everything you know, how you did certain things, how you behaved and nourished with time.

Secret # 26
Find time for yourself: Don't be too harsh on yourself; becoming a good parent does not mean you don't care about your well being. If you are happy with yourself, you can make your child happy.

Secret # 27
Don't spank: If you spank, your child will learn to become violent.
Mom & Dad: "Encourage me to finish my homework. Don't threaten me. It makes me dislike studies."

Secret # 28
Read your child: To understand your child, you need to understand child psychology. Try to analyse how your child feels and thinks. Respect his opinion too!

Secret # 29
Read books: There is a lot of research on parenting; read books on parenting and try to implement what you have learned. Mom & Dad: "When you show faith in me, it develops a lot of courage in me".

Secret # 30
Talk to other parents: Experienced parents will always have something important to tell you. Mom & Dad: "Give me little chores to do and help out at home. It teaches me life skills."

Secret # 31
Let them be: Don't ask your child to be someone; always encourage them to be themselves. Don't tell them to be like his friend Ravi," instead, help them be Shashank (your child's name).

Secret # 32
Understand your privilege: The child is a gift of God; understand your right as a parent. The child did not arrive at torture you, instead to make you happy.

Secret # 33
Please don't make them act like adults: A child grows into adults. It is a natural process. Let your child remain a child, don't expect them to act like adults. You don't expect an adult to behave like a child; why should you expect your child to act like an adult?

Secret # 34
Teach survival skills: Life is full of surprises; you never know what comes next. Therefore, make your child ready for various circumstances; for instance, teach them what to do when earthquakes come or when stranger approaches and alike.

Secret # 35
Let them learn: You are certainly more knowledgeable than your child, but your child is not ignorant; he has his intelligence. Let him know things in his ways. The more they know, the more they earn in life.

Secret # 36
Nurture your child's natural spirituality: Let your child grow naturally into his spiritual

understanding; let him learn from his surroundings. Practice Experiential Learning with the kids.

Secret # 37
Don't meddle: Do you like people meddling in your own business? Certainly not. A child has his world, don't create an atmosphere of meddling.

Secret # 38
Create a supportive atmosphere: Do you want your child to live in fear? Create an atmosphere where the child can do what he wants. Letting him do whatever he wants does not mean the child is allowed to commit wrongs all the time.

Secret # 39
Let the child be free: The thinking that you are his parent and you will never harm him has given birth to the thought that you should control your kids. Too much control is terrible, terrible.

Secret # 40

Give them true love: True love is not connected with showering your child with kisses or giving everything your child wants. True love means you are doing what is best for him.

Secret # 41
Create a loving atmosphere: If you are harsh on your child, he will never trust you; he might even hate you. Never compare your one child with the other. Each child is a creative genius.

Secret # 42
Teach your kids about TAXES!
Eat 30% of their ICE Cream.
Mom & Dad: "When I am throwing a huge tantrum, at times, all I need is a big hug."

Secret # 43
Don't boss around: Don't judge the child from an ivory tower; instead, sit below the child and try to understand his mind.

Secret # 44
Make yourself attractive: If you can attract your child, he will like you. When he wants you, he will follow you.

Secret # 45
Give love, take affection: Love is a two-way process; you need to give love if you want to be loved. Love your child, and he will shower with affection.

Secret # 46
Respect your child to be respected: Like love, respect is also a two-way process. If you respect your child, the child will certainly respect you.

Secret# 47
Spend quality time: To understand your child, you should spend quality time. If you spend quality time, you will also develop a friendship bond with your child.

Secret# 48
Manage your stress: Parenting can be very stressful. When you are too stressed out, you might be harsh on the child. Manage your stress, so don't spew your frustration on the child.

Secret # 49
Manage your anger: Most of us cannot avoid irritation; however, you need to control your anger when you are with your child. If you cannot stop yourself from slamming the door, your child will learn how to slam the door and when to slam the door.

Secret # 50
Develop a healthy relationship with your partner: A good parent is an individual who also has a good relationship with their partner. If you have a healthy relationship with your spouse, your child will grow in a healthy environment.

Secret # 51
Give them autonomy: The child is small yet has a distinct personality and individuality.

Secret # 52
Let them be independent: You are his parent, and you want your child to be the best; however, does the child want to do what you want him to do? Encourage the child to become self-reliant.

Secret # 53
Provide them opportunities: Let your child explore his hobbies, interests, and skills by giving them options.

Secret # 54
Provide a learning environment: Don t expect your child to pick up his textbook when switching the TV on.

Secret # 55
Generate good income: You need money to provide good education, upbringing, and medical bills.

Secret # 56
Save money: If you care about your child, you should start saving money and making plans for a better future.

Secret # 57
Behavioural management: Make punishment the last option. PunishmentDiscipline should be used only when all methods of behavioural

control have failed.

Secret # 58
Punish your child, but don't be too harsh: Research on parenting and child psychology tells that sometimes punishment is necessary to discipline the child, enforce rules, and encourage learning.

Secret # 59
Give them nutritious food: The child can be very selective about what they eat, encouraging them to eat healthy food.

Secret # 60
Maintain a healthy lifestyle: Go to bed early, and wake up early. Don't hang out late at night, and don't spend too much time at parties. How you live matters to your child.

Secret # 61
Exercise regularly: Teach your child the importance of exercise and take him jogging or cycling.

Secret # 62
Teach tolerance: we live in a multicultural society, and people from various cultures live among us. Teach your child how to appreciate people from other cultures.

Secret # 63
Teach religion: It is ok to encourage your child to participate in spiritual or religious activities; however, don't force religious guidance. Teach your kids to RESPECT All RELIGIONS.

Secret # 64
Keep an eye: out. You should be aware of your child's activities in school, after-school programs, and community activities.

Secret # 65
Know your child's friends: You should know your child's friends; you should know the parents of your child's friends. Your child's friend can tell you so many things about your child.

Secret # 66
Take precautions to protect your child: Danger is lurking around. Even a simple swing can be dangerous. Watch your child's back.

Secret# 67
Take the helm: Don't let the child dictate you. There will be no turning back once you play by his rules out of love. Therefore, let the child know you are in charge.

Secret # 68
Set a boundary: The world can be very confusing for your child; therefore, set a limit so that your child can explore his passion in a safe environment.

Secret # 69
Don't hurt his self-esteem: Your child is a distinct individual; he has his self-esteem. You don't want anyone to hurt your self-respect, do you?

Secret # 70

Don't clip your child's wings: If your child wants to do things like tying the shoelace, wearing the shirt etc., let him do it. This is good for you as well.

Secret# 71
Never try to fix everything. Let your child find his solution. Don't meddle until he gives up. By giving the child to find his answers, you are teaching him self-reliance and resilience.

Secret # 72
Discipline your child: Disciplining the child begins from home. You should make standard rules on what is allowed and not allowed.

Secret # 73
Remember discipline is not about exercising restrictions: Your child needs to be disciplined. However, punishment does not mean restricting them. Disciplining means letting them behave appropriately to become a good person.

Secret # 74
Discourage violence: Children are destructive by nature; they enjoy throwing things and breaking things. You should discourage violence

early on.

Secret # 75
Don't make too many rules: Children cannot absorb too many rules. Focus on the things that matter, such as study time, playtime and dinner time, with Tech-Candy Time on their priority!

Secret # 76
Don't be rude: If you are rude to your children, it is very likely to become rude to you. If you talk rudely, they will also speak rudely. If you behave rudely, children will also behave rudely.

Secret # 77
Be polite: Children will understand you when you are polite. If you are impolite, they may follow you initially; however, later, they will become a rebel.

Secret # 78
Understand the age group: Your child passes through various stages; you should understand these ages and treat them accordingly. Parenting a baby is different from parenting a

toddler.

Secret # 79
Treat them like a person: Children also have distinct personalities. They want respect, they want to be understood, and they want to be heard.

Secret # 80
Give them choices: You should not force your children to do want you to want them to do. Give them options; for instance, let them choose whether to read a storybook, play a video game or even enjoy their cloud presence!

Secret # 81
Spend quality time: Children want your time, want you to be around, and want you to participate in their activities. Therefore, you must have time for your children.

Secret # 82
Give them books: Books are the source of knowledge. Encourage children to read books. When they are reading, pick up your book and sit with them reading your book.

Secret # 83
Read aloud to children: You can encourage reading habits by reading aloud to your children. You read a paragraph and ask your child to read. Children love to listen to their parents. Reading together creates a bonding.

Secret # 84
Interact with the child: Interaction is the key to emotional development. You need to ask ququestionsquestions and get ready to answer your child's questions.

Secret # 85
Give them interactive toys: Interactive toys can entertain children and help them learn so many things. Things like building blocks will help them understand the alphabet and numerals.

Secret # 86
Schedule a play time: Children do not like seriousness; therefore, they are likely to watch cartoons instead of books. Schedule a playtime. You might tell them they can play the game once they finish breakfast.

Secret # 87
Let them see things: Seeing is believing. Instead of telling them what a tiger is or showing a video of a tiger, take them to the zoo and let them see a real tiger—experiential practice learning on routine.

Secret # 88
Go for co-parenting: Mother and father both have a responsibility to take care of the child. This is imperative for the emotional well-being of the child. Not just mothers but also fathers should take.

Secret # 89
Daddy time: Generally speaking, dads are most of the time not involved in parenting. Dads don't feed their children; they don't clean their children. Research tells kids taken care of by

dads to excel in school and develop problem-solving skills.

Secret # 90
Mummy time: In most cases, moms are the ones who are around the children all the time. This might bore the children. Moms should create special activities to engage children.

Secret # 91
Create warm memories: You sure have warm memories from your childhood, don't you? Do you remember when your day read stories to you? Do you remember when you and your mom played a board game?

Secret # 92
Create exciting activities: Boredom grabs children quickly. The toy they loved a week ago will no longer interest them. Create interesting activities. A simple thing like bathing a dog can be exciting to children or even watering the plants!

Secret # 93
Become a great cook: Children are very picky about what they eat. One of the common

problems for mothers is feeding their children. Learn cooking and always try new dishes.

Secret # 94

Let them enter the kitchen: Cooking is a fun activity for children. Your child will enjoy cooking with you. Don t let them play with a knife or go near the stove; however, you can ask them to beat the egg, sort out vegetables and arrange the table. Why not?

Secret# 95

Go for gardening: Children love to play with mud and water. Take them to the garden and help them sow the seeds, water the plants and explore nature!

Secret # 96

Bring a pet into your home: Children love animals and birds. Having a dog, a cat, a parrot, and even a fish in the house will make your children happy. Children love to interact with living things more than with non-living things like a toy cars.

Secret # 97
Admit your mistakes: When you admit your mistakes, your children will learn to apologise when they commit wrongs. Admitting your mistakes in front of your child will not diminish your personality.

Secret # 98
Go for a nature walk: Nature can teach a lot of things to your child. You can tell your child how trees help human beings, how humans depend on the ecosystem and even share the geography around!

Secret # 99
Teach them to care for the environment: Tell your child how the background relates to human beings. Teach them not to waste; tell them to reuse things. For example, you can tell him how water is essential and why he should not use wastewater.

Secret # 100
Encourage social responsibility: Picking trash from the garden might sound boring. However, your child might love this if you make this a

game.

Secret # 101
Teach them compassion: Help your child understand the power of kindness. Encourage them to be compassionate towards homeless people, animals and the poor.

Secret # 102
Always tell the truth: What kind of child you will bring up if you don't speak the truth? If you want your child to behave right, you should always talk about the fact. By telling the truth, you will be bringing a morally responsible individual.

Secret # 103
Don't lie to your child: If you continuously lie to your children, your child will stop believing you. If you lie, your child will no more respect you, no more love you. Even the white lies can be very damaging.

Secret # 104
Attend all the PTMs, School Functions, and Get Together moments at school without fail. When both MOM and DAD go to school together, the

kids love it!

Secret # 105
Don't nag with your partner: Children raised in families where partners quarrel will likely develop into a weak personalities. It is widespread to disagree with your partner. If you ever argue, always do it when the children are not around.

Secret # 106
Praise in public and criticise in Private. The same goes for your spouse and the kids! Remember this without fail!

Secret # 107
Respect your partner: In families where the women have a high opinion about their men and vice versa, the children will also have a lofty idea about their dads and moms. When you respect your partner, your child will more love his dad and mom.

Secret # 108
Respect the parenting differences: Your idea of

parenting might be different from your partner's idea. You need to support your spouse's parenting method because they do not mean any harm to the child.

Secret # 109
Praise your child: When your child does something good, praise him. When you praise them, he will be encouraged to do better. Even when he is not doing well, you have to praise him for attempting it.

Secret # 110
Always give positive feedback: A child needs positive feedback. Telling her that the drawing is crap will make her feel worse. Instead of saying the picture is terrible, you have to say, "If you erase this line and draw another curve here, the drawing will be better."

Secret # 111
Avoid negative feedback: Children are easily discouraged by negative feedback. When you give negative feedback, a child might lose interest in attempting the same thing again. Even if your child comes home with an "E" grade, don't give negative feedback on his face.

Secret # 112
Reward your child: Rewards significantly affect human psychology, even more on children. Reward your child for his achievement. You can tell him he will have a bicycle if he gets an "A" grade in the following exams.

Secret # 113
Cherish his achievements: Your child comes home with good grades; show your appreciation. If your child wins a trophy in a race, place the award alongside your valuables.

Secret # 114
Watch him perform: If your child participates in any competition, attend the event. If he makes it, hug him, kiss him. If he does not make it, praise him for participating.

Secret # 115
Make him feel special: Your child is very special to you; however, does your child know this? You have to make your child feel special each time and every time!

Secret # 116
Gossip about your child: It makes more sense when your child finds you saying good things about him to dad than in front of him.

Secret # 117
Trust Yourself: You know your child better than anyone; always trust your gut. Even if you think that you are wrong, you are likely correct.

Secret # 118
Know when to say YES and when to say NO: Disciplining a child can be adamant; you should know when to say yes and no.

Secret # 119
Say NO when your child is distrustful and intolerant: Don't let your child become disrespectful to you or anyone else. Stop him when he becomes intolerant.

Secret # 120
Build confidence: You can build confidence in your child by praising and rewarding his

achievements. You can also build confidence in the child by participating in his activities.

Secret # 121
Let him channelizechannelise emotions: If your child is angry, divert his mind by asking him to participate in exciting activities. If your child is crying, make him feel secure by hugging him tightly.

Secret # 122
Teach your kids
EMPATHY by telling them stories of your age/ life with moral lessons.

Secret # 123
Empower yourself with the power of TECHNOLOGY to match the requirements of the KIDS at home!

Secret # 124
Teach ethics: Teach your child what is ethical and what is unethical. Help him understand the difference between ethical and unethical.

Secret # 125
Teach morality: Morality distinguishes good and evil; character refers to er conduct. By teaching character, try to raise a morally responsible individual.

Secret # 126
Tell them the importance of values: Explain to your child why being good matters and how truthfulness will help in life.

Secret # 127
Don t fight when your child does not eat: Food fight is widespread. If your child does not eat a particular food, offer him another dish or ask him what he wants to eat. If he does not want to eat, let it be. Your child will not starve.

Secret # 128
Make a parenting schedule: parenting is hard work; it can exhaust you thoroughly. Making a schedule can ease your work. Set a timetable for various responsibilities.

Secret # 129
Encourage your kids to do creative things: Ask your child to sing, dance, write, draw, and play instruments. Creative activities like these will boost his mental capacity.

Secret # 130
Encourage physical activities: Research shows that brain development is connected with physical activity. Encourage your children to walk, run, and play outdoor games.

Secret # 131
Take your child to regular medical checkups: You should get all the required vaccines for your child. You also need to take your child to the doctor regularly. Never ignore the health-related complaints.

Secret # 132
Take care of personal hygiene: Encourage your child to brush their teeth, wash his hands and feet, and take a bath regularly. Learning should be made a habit rather than an occasional occurrence.

Secret # 133
Be vigilant about safety: Always make sure that the babies and toddlers are not left alone. Tell him to wear a helmet when riding his bike or scooter.

Secret # 134
Think twice before administering drugs: Antibiotics can cause problems; therefore, always look for alternatives.

Secret # 135
Promote independence: Your child's development will be hindered if he depends too much on you. You need to tell him that you are always with him, yet make him go alone.

Secret # 136
Never push too far: Have high expectations. Expect your child to do great things, tell him to aim high; however, never go too far.

Secret # 137
Let your child try: Resist doing what your child

can do herself. Your child might take 30 minutes to eat his meal by himself, and if you spoon-feed, you may do it in 10 minutes; however, by not letting your child do it on his own, you are hindering his learning process.

Secret # 138
Don't redo what your child has already done: Unless it is essential, don't fix what your child has already done. This will discourage your child from doing it on her own.

Secret # 139
Let them solve the problems: What do you do when you see your child trying to get a toy from the shelf that she finds hard to reach? If you want to get it for her, just stop.

Secret # 140
Give your child an assignment: Encourage your child to sort out the coloured dresses for the laundry, pick books from the floor, and choose the trash from the garden.

Secret # 141
Develop a routine: Make a routine for your child to read books, do his assignments, play games

and watch TV. Give them a say in your daily routine.

Secret # 142
Develop predictable routines: Children who follow the same way daily learn quickly. The training should include brushing teeth before going to bed, washing hands before eating and offering prayers at least once a day.

Secret # 143
Encourage cooperation: Make your child understand that human beings are social animals and that cooperation is the key to success. Teach teamwork by asking your child to get along with his peers.

Secret # 144
Teach manners: Children are deft in throwing tantrums. One of the ways to control tempers is by teaching them techniques. You have to teach them how to behave well.

Secret # 145
Make rules: You need to make rules and make

your child strictly follow these rules. The rules for the children can be as simple as "do not litter around" or as complex as "do not talk to the strangers."

Secret # 146
Be funny and humorous: Sometimes, you are required to make faces to make your child laugh, and sometimes you are required to dress funnily to make your child smile.

Secret # 147
Teach time management: You should teach your child when to stop watching TV, when to stop playing a video game and when to go to bed.

Secret # 148
Use infographics and images to teach your child: Research tells that children learn faster if infographics and images are used. Give them picture books to help them understand things.

Secret # 149
Let them watch instructional and educational videos: Children learn faster when they watch

instructional and educational videos.

Secret # 150
Use child-friendly language: Tell your child, "If you finish your homework, we might go to the park." Or, "Finish your homework, we'll go to the park." You can see the difference in reactions.

Secret # 151
Don t use vulgar words: Never use curse words or obscene words in front of the child. No "shit", no "IDIOT". Make them aware of the signs of CHILD ABUSE too!

Secret # 152
Don t compare your child with another child: Jealousy and enmity will develop when you begin to compare your child with another child.

Secret # 153
Have a movie time: Everyone needs entertainment? Take your child to the movie, or have a movie time in the home.

Secret # 154
Play music: Music will unburden your exhausted mind and make your child happy.

Secret # 155
Encourage teamwork: What if children are fighting over the same toy? You can tell one child to play for 10 minutes and then give it to another to play for 10 minutes.

Secret # 156
Let your child settle his dispute: If the children are debating, don't interfere unless one of them goes violent. Let the children resolve their conflicts.

Secret # 157
Learn how to divert your child's mind. If your child is drawing on the wall, bring chart paper and ask him to remove it from the form.

Secret # 158
Learn to manage good-bye meltdowns: Your child may not want to leave you and go to

school. Give him something like your picture, a heart-shaped tissue to make him feel that you are with him.

Secret # 159
Help them in righting their wrongs: When your child tears papers and throws them over the floor, ask him to collect the pieces and throw them in the dustbin. Make " Sorry" and "Thank you" their favourite language.

Secret # 160
Reprimand immediately: If your child does something wrong, reprimand immediately. Don't wait until you get home.

Secret # 161
Make sure they get enough sleep: Children are very proactive; they need rest. Research says if a sixth grader child loses one hour of sleep, his intelligence will be reduced to that of a fourth-grader.

Secret # 162
Raise honest kids: Honesty is the best policy is an old saying. However, research has proved that he will grow up into a responsible human

being when a child is real. Your child might lie to please you or get benefits. Always check whether the child is telling the truth or not.

Secret # 163
You need rules: Kids need directions, and so do you. Setting rules for kids also mean you have your own rules to follow. If you don't want your kid to watch TV late at night, you also need to avoid watching TV late.

Secret # 164
Too much control is terrible: The kids whose parents are too strict are the ones who do drugs, drink and smoke. Never do so in front of them ever too!

Secret # 165
Don't let boredom get into your child: Your child might be bored if you are too busy for your child. When a child is bored, he will try to take refuge in activities such as smoking, drinking, and drugs.

Secret # 166

Get into healthy arguments: Research has shown that reasonable opinion positively affects children.

Secret # 167
Teach them to be grateful: Being grateful is excellent quality. Your children must learn how to express gratitude.

Secret # 168
Create the right atmosphere: You need to have a child-friendly environment in your house. Creating the right atmosphere is a big part of parenthood. The right atmosphere implies happiness, love, compassion, and discipline.

Secret # 169
Don't impose your dream: You might have wanted to become a doctor but ended by being a salesperson. Don't put pressure on your child to fulfil your dream.

Secret # 170
Know what the child needs: You have a business and see your child as your successor. This is

quite reasonable. However, does your child want to follow in your footsteps?

Secret # 171
Don't pamper: It is true that you need to make your child feel special. However, if you are too much bragging about your child, you are spoiling him.

Secret # 172
Be ready to learn from your child: As a parent, you are the first teacher to your child. However, there are so many things that your child can teach you. Having a child means you are ready to learn so many things.

Secret # 173
Be joyful: Nobody forced you to become a parent; it was your ce. If you show tension, anger, fear, anxiety, and jealousy now and then, what will the child learn?

Secret # 174
Improving behavioural problems in children: Toddlers show tantrums, and teens are rebellious by nature. You cannot solve the behavioural issues in children until you

understand their minds and know what exactly they want. Communicate as much as you can to sort out the problems.

Secret # 175
Learn how to entertain the children: If you can keep the children busy, you will win the battle to keep them quiet. There are various ways to engage your child; find out what's your child's favourite.

Secret # 176
Go for outings: Like you, children get bored with routine life, then go on tour to make life enjoyable. This will also create a deep bonding.

Secret # 177
OrganizeOrganise children's parties: To show how much you love him, you need to organise children's parties and invite your child's friends. Parties are suitable for the children and parents as they encourage social interactions amongst the parents.

Secret # 178

Check the development process: Make sure you are aware of the changes in your children's bodies. Guide them about the changes in their personality and character and impart to them about SEX EDUCATION before learning from the outside world.

Secret # 179

Check the learning process: Find out how your child is learning. Look into his notebooks, school reports and homework. Never guide them to their homework directly. Have an eye on their study routine.

Secret # 180

Find out if someone is bullying your child: Bullying can be detrimental to mental development. Find out whether your child is being bullied in the neighbourhood or at school.

Secret # 181

Find out whether your child is struggling with cyberbullying: It is widespread to see children as young as five years use the internet. Check for the signs of cyberbullying.

Secret # 182

Check your children's online activities: The Internet is a source of information and knowledge. However, there are also many bad things over the internet. Be aware of their user IDs and Passwords. A Good Parent is a Friend of their kids on Social Networking Sites.

Secret # 183
Exercise parental control on cable TV: TV is a good source of learning and entertainment. However, TV also brings channels that can harm the child.

Secret # 184
Exercise parental control on the internet: You need to block malicious sites to stop children from checking porn sites and other illegal sites.

Secret # 185
Don to let them choose friends over parents: Children will always go to their friends when it comes to confiding something. However, their friends are not the best people to give them advice. You can be your childhood friends and encourage them to confide in you.

Secret # 186
Let them choose their career: You know what is best for your children. However, what you think is the best might not be the best for them. Advise them, but let them take their path.

Secret # 187
Make yourself available: You must always be open when your children need you. One mistake can damage their entire life. Respect your parents before your KIDS.

Secret # 188
Don make them feel they can have it all: Don'take things easier for your kid. They need to understand things are also not easier for parents.

Secret # 189
Teach the value of money: Money has—great importance in life. Teach your children it is not easy to make money. If you are giving pocket money, check how they are spending it.

Secret # 190
Teach them to spend less and save more: If they learn how hard it is to make money, they will learn the importance of spending less and saving more.

Secret # 191
Happy families, do. Happen by accident. They are born from intentional parenting. Make sure you as a parent value the family meal and car rides.

Secret # 192
Learn to move on: One day, your child becomes a teen and is ready to leave the house (for work, education etc.). Whether he is one month old or 50 years old, your child is your child.

Secret # 193
Don't compromise your wellbeing: Your children are your blood and bones. However, you should never compromise your well-being. Taking care of children does not mean you have to forget about yourself.

Secret # 194

You don't own your children: One of the main issues of conflict between the parents and children is the sense of ownership in parents. Parents tend to think their children like their pets. Give them freedom of life.

Secret # 195

Get support from others: There is no five-point guide to parenting. Everyone has their writing style. If you have difficulty, you can join a parent's group and ask for help.

Secret # 196

Raise a giver: There is so much pleasure in giving. Teach your child to become a giver. Let your child understand the importance of giving. Remember, YOU just can not raise as you were raised!

Secret # 197

Don't let them get away with meanness: Children can be very mean. They are likely to do emotional blackmailing. Be involved in their lives.

Secret # 198
Ask your kids to help you: When you need extra hands for household work, ask your children to volunteer. This will make your children respond to the family's needs. Frequently ask them to do Car Wash or water the plants together.

Secret # 199
Don't yell: Generally speaking, yelling will produce a parent-deaf kid. This shall also cause a dislike with either of the parents by the kid for life.

Secret # 200
Move close, but give them privacy: You need to be close to your kids and provide them with privacy. Know their friends and observe their routine. Never bridge their interest but feed their likes. Reduce stress by celebrating successes, no matter how small. This has to be a priority by any means.

About The Author

Dheeraj Mehrotra, MS, MPhil, PhD (Education Management) honoris causa., a white and a yellow belt in SIX SIGMA, a Certified NLP Business Diploma holder, is an Educational Innovator, Author, with expertise in Six Sigma In Education, Academic Audits, Neuro-Linguistic Programming (NLP), Total Quality Management In Education, an Experiential Educator, a CBSE Resource towards School Assessment (SQAA), CCE, JIT, Five S, and KAIZEN. He has authored over 40 books on Computer Science for ICSE/ ISC/ CBSE Students, over 60 books of academic interest for the field of education excellence, and Six Sigma. A former Principal at De Indian Public School, New Delhi, (INDIA) with an ample teaching experience of over Two Decades, he is a certified Trainer for Quality Circles/ TQM in Education and QCI Standards for School Accreditation/ Six Sigma in Education. He has also been honoured with the President of India's National Teacher Award in the year 2006 and the Best Science Teacher State Award (By the Ministry of Science and Technology, State of UP), Innovation in Education for his inception of Six Sigma In Education by Education Watch, New Delhi and Education World- Best Teacher Award, BOLT Learner Teacher Award by Air India, 'Innovation in Education Award 2016' by Higher Education Forum (HEF), Gujarat Chapter, among others. He has developed over 150 FREE EDUCATIONAL MOBILE Apps for the Google Play Store exclusively for Teachers, Students, and Parents. This work has been recognized by the LIMCA BOOK OF RECORDS & INDIA BOOK OF RECORDS as the only Indian to draw that feast. Dr Mehrotra is presently working as a PRINCIPAL at KUNWARS GLOBAL SCHOOL, Lucknow, in India. He has conducted over 1000 workshops globally on "Excellence In Education" integrated with Total Quality Management and Six Sigma, Technology Integration in Education (TIE), Developing towards being ROCKSTAR TEACHERS, including Cyberspace, Cyber Security, Classroom Management, School Leadership & Management, and Innovative teaching within classrooms via Mind Maps, NLP and Experiential Learning in Academics. He is an active TEDx speaker and can be viewed on the youtube TEDx channel.As a premium UDEMY Instructor, he has also developed over 450 courses and is catering to over 8 Lakh students from 180 plus countries. He can be visited atwww.authordheerajmehrotra.com

Books By The Same Author

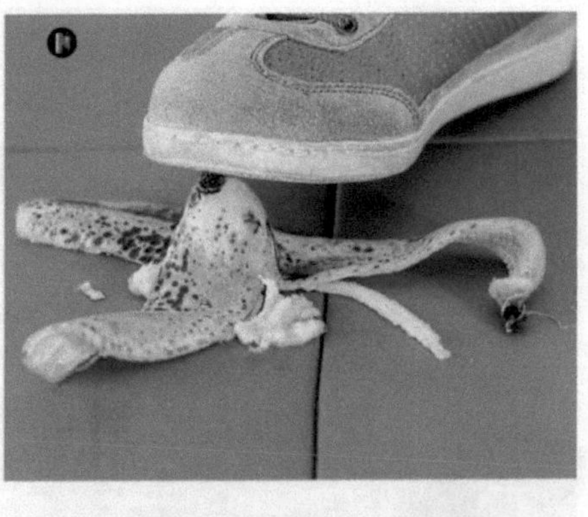

SECURING SAFETY & QUALITY CARING

99 SAFETY AND SECURITY

ANCHORS WITHIN SCHOOLS

DR. DHEERAJ MEHROTRA

A PRIORITY

FOR SCHOOLS

www.authordheerajmehrotra.com

BOOKS BY THE SAME AUTHOR

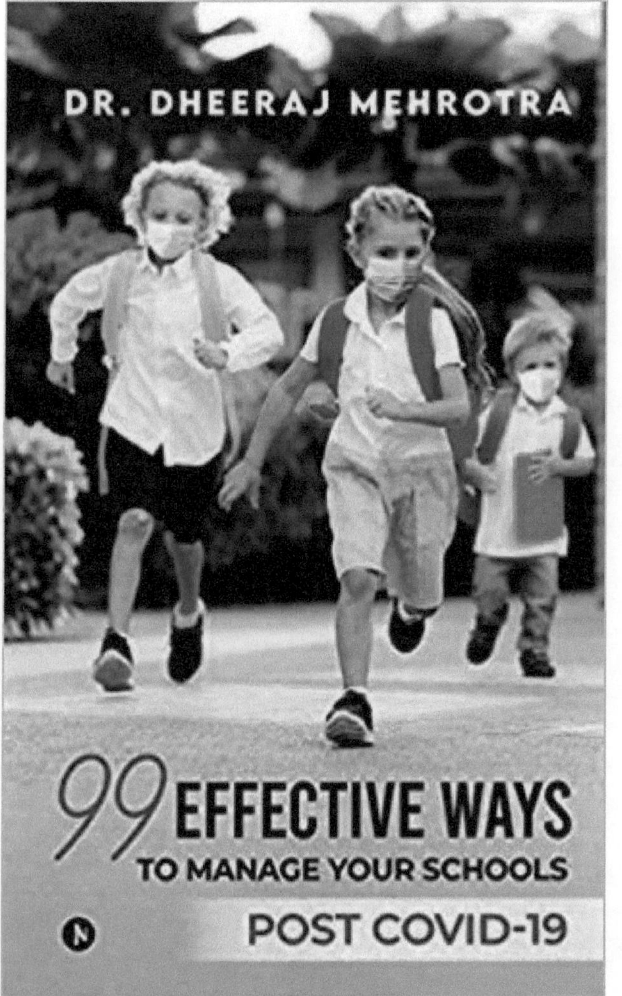
DR. DHEERAJ MEHROTRA
99 EFFECTIVE WAYS
TO MANAGE YOUR SCHOOLS
POST COVID-19

9 798887 045603

Printed by Libri Plureos GmbH in Hamburg,
Germany